ALSO BY DR. JAMES A. HAMBRICK

Holiness in an Unholy Society
Godly Living in Perilous Times

RED, WHITE, AND TRUE

Living Your Faith in the
Workplace in America

James A. Hambrick, PhD

WESTBOW PRESS
A DIVISION OF THOMAS NELSON
& ZONDERVAN

Unless otherwise indicated, all scripture taken from the New
King James Version. Copyright 1979, 1980, 1982 by Thomas
Nelson, Inc. Used by permission. All rights reserved.

WestBow Press books may be ordered through booksellers or by contacting:

WestBow Press
A Division of Thomas Nelson & Zondervan
1663 Liberty Drive
Bloomington, IN 47403
www.westbowpress.com
1 (866) 928-1240

ISBN: 978-1-4908-2703-2 (sc)

Library of Congress Control Number: 2014903090

Printed in the United States of America.

WestBow Press rev. date: 02/13/2014

In loving memory of our Heroes

Sgt. Jerry Mundy

Mt. Juliet Police Department

&

Deputy John Musice

Wilson County Sheriff's Office

(End of Watch: 07/09/2003)

"Therefore, the prisoner of the Lord, beseech you to have a walk worthy of the calling with which you were called."

(Ephesians 4:1)

CONTENTS

PREFACE

Wow! What an amazing service that we had on Sunday. The Spirit was high, the choir was awesome, and the word went forth in a powerful way. We were so blessed! (Now fast forward 15 hours, the alarm clock goes off). Man, I can't believe its Monday already, I have to get up and go into work. "I hate Mondays" many have been heard to say or maybe you've said it yourself. Now you get up and get prepared for the day on the job and somehow, all of the jubilation of Sunday is gone, forgotten, or suppressed far back in your memory, even though not even 24 hours has passed. You get to work and nothing seems to be going right, you're frustrated and others can tell. Your testimony is being challenged. People know that you go to church every Sunday, they have heard you talk about what a good time you have and you have even invited many of them to visit and worship with you. But the character that you display on the job is not lining up with the words that they sometimes hear from you.

This book is a work that challenges us to a walk of faith, not only on Sunday in the church house, but also in our everyday lives and on our jobs. There are many who believe that our place of employment is no place for our faith, they believe that there is a "separation between church and state." So they make a conscious effort not to come across as been a "holy roller," and not to offend anyone with their belief. I don't want anyone to think that I am saying that we should be so dogmatic in our belief as to beat people over the head with our faith, but I am saying that people should know us and identify us as being a people of faith. It should not only be expressed on Sunday morning or whenever your day of worship is. There is freedom and liberty in Christ, and He wants us to live freely in our expression of Him and for Him. Christianity is a 24/7, 365 days commitment. A commitment to a God centered life at church, home, school, and the workplace. I encourage you as Paul states, "Imitate me as I imitate Christ." That should be our attitude and our model. We are to go out into the world and make disciples; we are to go fishing for men, what better place could there be than at our workplace. Remember, Jesus said that the harvest is plentiful, but the laborers are few. Let's rise up and be a faithful laborer in the workplace in America!

ACKNOWLEDGEMENTS

I would like to give thanks to God Almighty, The Lord Jesus Christ, and The Holy Spirit for their leading and inspiration of this work. To my wife for her selfless sacrifice, understanding, encouragement, and motivation to complete it. To my entire family for the love and support. To my co-workers, co-laborers in ministry and all saints who are not ashamed of their faith. Finally, to the families of Jerry Mundy and John Musice for their continued friendship. This book is dedicated to Jerry and John, for their bravery, service, and their lives which will never be forgotten.

-James

INTRODUCTION

Stop! Police, Stop! And the chase is on. Adrenaline has kicked in, getting the bad guy is the focus and the pursuit is relentless; behind the dark buildings, through the thick woods, now the back yards, the barking of dogs, the sweat running profusely from the face, slipping in the mud you fall, but you get up and keep going; now you are tiring, but you press on, and finally you get your man. You handcuff the suspect, walk back to the patrol unit, and transport him to booking. The reports are taken and you go back to the beat; why? The answer is, because we've have been called to do it!

Many have only watched this play out on their television sets, but we live it; from Mayberry to Southland our profession like many others has been glamorized and criticized. There's a saying that nobody wants the police around until they are a victim of some crime. Underpaid, underappreciated, nasty stares, and negative criticism, for what? The answer is we've been called to do it! Protect and serve is our motto, we are the enforcers in this unholy society that I wrote about in my last book. We kiss our families goodbye like everyone else does, but with this calling comes added risk, yet we take it in stride. We have a job to do; someone will complain, someone will say they didn't deserve the citation and will give all kinds of excuses and might even curse you out; but you take it and go on. Why? The answer is we've been called to do it.

At the end of the day it's about going home to the ones that really love and appreciate us. It's about being able to hold your wife, husband, son, or daughter; and though we provide a stable income for the household, we have an understanding that it's more than that; often times it's hard to explain why we like doing what we do, but more than anything else, we do it because we are called to do it. There is something that is rewarding in the vocation and though many times we are not appreciated. There are those times when we are, and it makes it all worth it, to help someone, to see a little child's eyes light up when they see the uniform, it feels good. To know that someone cares makes a difference and keeps us focused and willing to serve so that we can get the "bad guy". Why? Because we've been called to do it!

This book is about living your faith in the midst of your occupation in America. Even though there will be a primary focus on the law enforcement community, it is not only for law enforcement. It is anyone who is living out their faith in the workplace, and a call for those who are not to get on board! We will discuss the challenges of this and the rewards of it as well. There have been interviews with people in various areas of employment, from patrol officers, to administrators, both sworn and non-sworn personnel, chaplains, educators, musicians, bankers and other occupations. And most importantly, those who's loved ones paid the ultimate price in the line of duty. So take the journey with me as we travel the RED, WHITE, and TRUE!

SECTION I

OUR AUTHORITY

"Let every soul be subject to the governing authorities. For there is no authority except from God, and the authorities that exist are appointed by God. Therefore whoever resists the authority resists the ordinance of God, and those who resist will bring judgment on themselves. Rulers are not a terror to good works, but to evil. Do you want to be unafraid of the authority? Do what is good, and you will have praise from the same.

He is God's minister to you for good. But if you do evil, be afraid; for he does not bear the sword in vain; for he is God's minister, an avenger to execute wrath on him who practices evil. Therefore you must be subject, not only because of thee wrath but also for conscience' sake. For because of this you also pay taxes, for they are God's ministers attending continually to this very thing. Render therefore to all their due: taxes to whom taxes are due, customs to whom customs, fear to whom fear, honor to whom honor."(Romans 13:1-7)

The police academy, the swearing in ceremony, or maybe the initial sit down talk with the chief, were possibly where you believed the authority to protect and serve came from; but I submit to you that we have authority, and it comes from a source that it much higher than these. Our authority comes from a supreme and sovereign source, it comes from the one who created all things; it is from the one who instituted governments and law, it comes from Almighty God! He is the author and finisher of it all. This is a truth that many have not come to understand or realize; though one may be unsaved and not have a relationship with the Lord, still, he has given the authority to the position in which they serve which makes them operate under a divine banner. This is not only true for law enforcement, but government as a whole. From the policeman to the president, the appointment is under the direction of God. The word declares that they are God's ministers.

I realize that this may be hard to grasp for some given different events in our time such as the Rodney King case or the beating of several men in Philadelphia, PA., or similar cases involving police brutality or misconduct of the office. We see the stories of the officer that has gone "rogue" by stealing, selling drugs, or doing some other crime, and when we see it, it's hard to identify that they are God's minister. We must understand that the authority is given to the office, so the word says that if we want to be unafraid of the authority, do good and you will have praise of the same. We will talk more about this later because I feel that this is certainly an area where we can improve. I will discuss the reasons why there may be a lacking of praise from the officers when people are doing the right thing.

This profession is an honorable one; it is one where the stressors and demands can be high, while the pay and benefits are low. One would probably ask, why in the world would anyone want to do it? The answer remains, because we are called to do it. You will hear from others in the profession as we go along in this book that will help in knowing about the people in the profession because there are many that fail to realize that we are real people with real feelings and emotions that live life like everyone else, that experience life challenges and have to make life choices like everyone else. We will explore the impact of such challenges on our lives as well as try to understand the dynamics of introducing our faith walk in the midst of it all. How many times have you heard the term "Bad Cop"? I submit to you that there are good and bad in any occupation, and not just in police officers. The problem is police officers are continually lumped into one pile, and when one messes up, we are all guilty of the infraction. Go to McDonalds, you will find good and bad employees, when you go to the stores to shop, or to the movies to be entertained you will find individuals that do a good job and those who don't. Law enforcement is no different, while I tell you that it is a calling, there are those who get into it for the wrong reasons, and more often than not, they don't last long. Eventually these individuals quit or get into some kind of trouble and are terminated for one reason or another. They are the ones that do the job with the wrong motivation and are there just to make a paycheck. Ask a real officer about their motivation and I can tell you they are in it because they have a heart for the work that they have been called to do.

In the occupation of law enforcement, we encounter people, usually at some bad time or point in their life. It is normally at a time of trouble where they have been victimized in one type of situation or another, but often it's a bad time in their life. Through these experiences, the officer has to be different things to different people, and by that I mean; we become for some a rescuer, a mentor, a counselor, a protector, a listening ear, and even a shoulder to cry on. For others, we are the threat to their business or addiction; we are the bad guys that are taking a father or a mother from a child or a husband or wife from their spouse. We are often labeled as the ones that don't understand what people are going through and are insensitive with no hearts, so we are called every kind of name in the book for just doing what we have been called to do.

The real fact of the matter is, law enforcement officers have much heart and much compassion and it is demonstrated by many of the actions that we do on a daily basis. When most people get off from work they are able to go sit around and talk about their day with others; in law enforcement I can tell you that that is a rare thing. We see so much within the scope of our occupation and most of the time we want to forget it so most push it deep down and even suppress the experience. Most of us do not go home and talk about the job because we don't want to bring our spouse's into the same mindset. Right or wrong, this is how it really is, and so there are many that try to escape it all with alcohol or some other vice. These are the challenges to living out our faith in the area of law enforcement, and the overall workplace in America.

CHAPTER ONE

INTEGRITY

The American Heritage Dictionary defines integrity as; "steadfast adherence to a strict moral or ethical code." In the workplace this can be as simple as honoring your word. Another definition is; "making the correct choice when faced with right and wrong." It further encompasses adherence to ethics and morals, and is often linked with honesty. Integrity is of utmost importance especially in the workplace. It speaks to the type of person you are and if you can be trusted to do the job, or perform the assignment that you've been tasked to do. You have to understand that in life there are going to be challenges, and there are going to be times of temptations that you are presented with. The question is; will you be able to overcome the temptation and integrity to shine, or will you cave in to the pressures that many allow themselves to be robbed by.

From the beginning of the creation of mankind we have been presented with the opportunity to make a choice between right and wrong, or god and evil. Ever since the temptation and fall of Adam in the garden, we have been tempted to do evil and make bad decisions. This is magnified when the ability and frequency in ones occupation is prevalent, such as the case in the law enforcement profession. In our current news is a story of a former officer being indicted on charges of the conspiracy to transport a large amount of cocaine using his patrol vehicle, and another for theft, bribery, and drug charges. Any law enforcement officer can point to a time or incident where the opportunity was presented for them to take advantage of a situation or individual. A traffic stop, or call to a residence, or one of many other responses that are associated with the job; there was the time for a decision between doing right or doing wrong. There was the chance to walk in integrity. I believe that most officers make the right choice and walk honorable when faced with these decisions, however, as we all know by our news media, there are the ones that don't and it puts a mark on law enforcement in general. Integrity is a vital part and attribute of the law enforcement officer and other occupations as well. When our agency is conducting interviews for employment I ask each candidate "what does integrity mean to you?" some give the answer that I'm looking for while others act like it's something they never heard of. Police integrity is a serious topic that has been the spotlight of law enforcement concern for the last fifteen to twenty-five years. Corruption and integrity are germane, where corruption is basically dishonesty for personal gain and integrity can be best defined as "The normaltive inclination among police to resist temptations to abuse the rights and privileges of their occupation" (U.S. Department of Justice, 2005). Integrity can be measured based upon an individual's moral principles or ethical values. The opportunity to demonstrate integrity not only exists in the area of law enforcement, but in every occupation. There are times when you may be tempted in some form or another in the work place and it's during these times when your true character will shine. You see, someone gave a simple definition of integrity saying, "Integrity is doing the right thing even when no one is around". Look at this scenario; you stop a vehicle for suspicion of the driver being intoxicated, or as we say, "for DUI"; after the stop is made, you get the driver out of the vehicle so that he can perform some field sobriety task. The driver is so intoxicated that he has a hard time standing, let alone perform any task, so you handcuff him and put him in your patrol car. Now you go and check the vehicle for alcohol, drugs, a weapon etc; in the process you see some money folded in the middle console, its three hundred dollars. Now you have a choice to make, list it on the inventory sheet and secure it with the other property that will be listed or you could say "man this guy is so wasted that he won't even remember anything, besides, it's my word against his". What would you do? Nobody is around, it's a good lick and you can use the money. A person with integrity does the right thing and logs the money down as inventory.

This is just one scenario that is probably played out hundreds of thousands of times each year in this country, its real and there are many more like it where we are presented with an opportunity to do right or wrong.

Now we introduce into the conversation men and women who have a relationship with the Lord Jesus Christ. They work in the same conditions and are presented with the same challenges and opportunities. They have the same DUI scenario played out before them constantly, but it's something about them that is different. I'm not saying that they can't be tempted, I am saying that the decision of what to do is less challenging because while they are at the work place they are constantly living out their faith. They understand that integrity is a must, and that they are accountable to God for their actions, because, even though people may not be watching, he is always watching. And in the midst of their daily lives and occupation we want to please him.

I have heard of many instances where a law enforcement officer gave into the temptations of the job and is now paying dearly for it. As I stated earlier, the law enforcement profession is an honorable one, not because of the individuals who serve, but because of the one who ordained it, Almighty God! He knows about temptation, when His Son walked this earth there are recorded times where He was tempted. The writer of the New Testament book Hebrews records this; *"For we do not have a High Priest who cannot sympathize with our weaknesses, but was in all points tempted as we are, yet without sin." (Hebrews 4:15)* By this we can see that we are without excuse, because the Son of God walked this earth as a man, and as a man was tempted just as we are, yet He did not give into the temptation. I have heard some say, "well that's just because He was God", I say it doesn't matter because God has also given us the Holy Spirit to lead, guide and protect us. If we are sensitive enough to hear the Holy Spirit when He is speaking to us we will make the right decisions, if we are obedient to His voice. And believe me; He speaks to us even in the midst of our occupations.

It may be challenging for anybody, but I feel it is especially tough for those without a relationship with God through His Son Jesus Christ. It's sad that we continue to hear of incidents where an officer finds himself on the other end or the wrong side of the law by doing various things like taking money off of individuals for their personal gain. I've even heard of officers robbing Hispanic individuals by making traffic stops for some reason and then taking their money. Someone that walks in integrity would not do this, no matter how alone they think they may be. We as law enforcement officers have to do better, we must do better! Remember in the age of technological advances, it seems as though someone is always watching, but even with that said I would have you to understand that God is always watching. Psalm 15 gives us a look at integrity in daily living; *"Lord, who may abide in Your tabernacle? Who may dwell in Your holy hill? He who walks uprightly, and works righteousness, and speaks truth in his heart; He who does not backbite with his tongue, nor does evil to his neighbor, nor does he take up a reproach against his friend; In whose eyes a vile person is despised, but he honors those who fear the Lord; He who swears to his own hurt and does not change, he who does not put out his money at usury, nor does he take a bribe against the innocent. He who does these things shall never be moved". (Psalm 15:1-5)*

CHAPTER TWO

RELIABILITY

Can you be counted on? At home with your family are you the one that brings some level of stability because of the fact that they can count on you? Are you reliable? Can you be counted on by your co-workers or the members of your community? Reliability is a critical asset of an individual. It gives a sense of comfort and security for one to know that they can count on you. We often say that it's good to know when someone has your back. Is it a part of your character? While there is an important place in our relationships with one another as it relates to reliability, the bigger question is; can God count on you? Does He view you as being reliable? Reliability is defined as "the quality or state of being reliable", it also speaks to the area of consistency.

Here enters the very essence of this writing, in the framework of your occupation, are you living or modeling a life that glorifies God in the midst of the workplace. There are many that have no problem with proclaiming Christ on Sunday at church, but struggle with it during the week and especially on their jobs. It seem as though they are ashamed of the Lord or their faith, they express as though they are Sunday only Christians. Many feel that their faith has no place in the workplace and try to attach the label that there should be a separation of church and state. The enemy gets a lot of mileage in the workplace because we fail the Lord in the area of being reliable to live lives that glorify Him in the workplace.

We must understand that the Lord has done so much for us and we have a responsibility to carry out His mission even while we are involved in our careers. What if the Lord treated us like we treat Him? You see, we want the blessings of God, we want to experience the love of God, and we have no problem asking Him for something that we want or need. But when it's time for us to represent Him, we somehow come up with all kinds of excuses why we should keep our faith segregated from our daily lives. In the book of Romans we find the words of the Apostle Paul; though he was in a place that was really somewhat hostile he said; *"For I am not ashamed of the gospel of Christ, for it is the power of God to salvation for everyone who believes, for the Jew first and also for the Greek." (Romans 1:16)*

So the question that needs to be answered is; are we ashamed of Christ, and our faith? Do we not realize that The God of Sunday is the God of the rest of the week? The mission that He has given us is an everyday mission. Notice to this point I have not said anything about preaching or speaking Christ, I have been more concerned about our living Christ in every aspect of our life, including the workplace. We must show ourselves to be reliable to God, because I know for a fact that we can count on Him for what we need.

Remember, reliability means following through on our commitments, doing what we say we will do. When we are reliable, others can count on us, and we can count on ourselves. Reliability is one of the foundations of teamwork or cooperation. It allows people to work together, with each person doing what he or she does best, knowing that friends, family, or co-workers are taking care of other tasks. Listen to a couple of quotes that relate to liability; "The shifts of fortune test the reliability of friends" –Marcus T. Cicero. "Lots of people want to ride with you in the limo, but what you really want is someone who will take the bus with you when the limo breaks down"-Oprah Winfrey.

So I'll ask the question another way; how consistent are you in the area of reliability? I pray that we will all get to the point where we answer, Very!

"You have tested my heart; You have visited me in the night; You have tried me and found nothing; I have purposed that my mouth shall not transgress. Concerning the works of men, By the word of Your lips, I have kept myself from the path of the destroyer.

(Psalm 17:3-4)

SECTION II

OUR PURPOSE

EDUCATION INFOGRAPHIC ELEMENTS

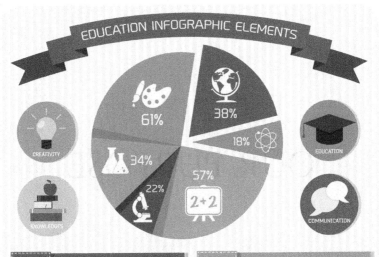

CREATIVITY

EDUCATION

KNOWLEDGES

COMMUNICATION

61%

38%

18%

34%

57%

22%

2 + 2

01 Lorem ipsum qui dolore sit amete, consectetur adipisicing panatur elit, sed do eiusmod tempor incididunte ut labore et ex dolore magna aliqua.

04 Lorem ipsum qui dolore sit amete, consectetur adipisicing panatur elit, sed do eiusmod tempor incididunte ut labore et ex dolore magna aliqua.

02 Lorem ipsum qui dolore sit amete, consectetur adipisicing panatur elit, sed do eiusmod tempor incididunte ut labore et ex dolore magna aliqua.

05 Lorem ipsum qui dolore sit amete, consectetur adipisicing panatur elit, sed do eiusmod tempor incididunte ut labore et ex dolore magna aliqua.

03 Lorem ipsum qui dolore sit amete, consectetur adipisicing panatur elit, sed do eiusmod tempor incididunte ut labore et ex dolore magna aliqua.

06 Lorem ipsum qui dolore sit amete, consectetur adipisicing panatur elit, sed do eiusmod tempor incididunte ut labore et ex dolore magna aliqua.

CHAPTER THREE

SERVICE

We have an awesome privilege and responsibility in life and in the workplace; it doesn't matter what occupation you do or feel that you are called to, you have an opportunity to serve. Everyone from the newest entry level person to the CEO has an obligation for service. We were not created to occupy time and space, we were created for purpose, and service is a part of that purpose. There are many that live as though service is not a part of their vocabulary; they want to be served rather serve. First we must understand that we were created for the purpose of serving God, and our fellow man. None of us are on an island to live lives unto ourselves.

One of the ways we serve God is by serving others. There are many areas of service, and we can find our place in and through some of them. God created each of us in His image and with uniqueness that only He could do. So we must find our service within our own uniqueness. When this is done it won't be a chore to serve, but we will, and should recognize it for what it is, and that is, a blessing! Referring to His purpose, Jesus stated; ***"Now My soul is troubled, and what shall I say? Father, save me from this hour? But for this purpose I came to this hour." (John 12:27)*** He knew His purpose for coming down from heaven, for suffering for humanity, for dying a horrible death on the cross for sin, even though He was sinless. And though He knew what He had to do, it was not an easy thing; so we hear in His prayer to the Father, "save me from this hour". Taking on the sin of humanity was an awesome responsibility. And in the hour of death He would be separated for the first time from the Father. He was obedient in service, even the death of the cross, for you and me.

What will you sacrifice in the arena of service? What are you willing to give? A life of service requires a life of giving. You can give in many ways that will bring glory and honor to the Lord. I'm not talking about giving just in monetary terms, but the giving of yourself. This can be demonstrated in a number of ways. Remember there is a great blessing in the small things of service, and there is also great sense of gratification that comes in serving. In the occupation of law enforcement, you may be familiar with the motto "to protect and serve". Often we may see this on the side of a police cruiser of a particular police department, but this slogan goes further than just police officer. We will talk about the protection part in a moment, but for now let's continue to focus on the serving part. Many people go about their day in their various jobs without considering that they are there to serve. Take for instance, an employee that is solely out for the paycheck, we see these individuals go about the day as though the world owes them something. In their world it's all about them and not about anyone else. For example, I have heard of officers that get beside themselves when someone simply asks for directions. They respond with smart comments like; "do I look like a roadmap?" The person usually is asking because they feel if anyone knows the area it's probably an officer. Where is the service in this type of attitude and behavior? We should consider the "GOLDEN RULE" wherever we are in life, be it the workplace or marketplace. "Do onto others as you would have them do unto you." This is certainly a good rule to live by, and think on when we are faced with many of life's decisions.

Service starts with an attitude. Having a heart to do for someone else, and treating them like you would want to be treated. A life of service requires a life of patience. You will need to be patient at various times when you are helping others. Many people will attempt to hurry when they are dealing with other people, they have this air about them that suggests that you are wasting their time or invading their space. They hurry up so they can get back to other things and often feel that you are a distraction.

Trust me; I know that every day is not a sunny day in one's life. There are those days when we would rather just stay in the bed. It is in those times when we really need to pray for God's strength to help us through the day, and draw encouragement from the blessing of helping someone else. No matter what line of work you are in, from doctor or lawyer, teacher or preacher, banker or baker, every one of us are presented with opportunities to serve others. But when we actually take the time to put other's requirements before our own, we get an opportunity to step away from the internal chatter of what we need and get to something else. We get to something better. Not only do we find success, we find a new kind of happiness. I'm sure you've experienced one of those extraordinary moments of service at your job. It's the kind of thing that stands out when you spend your days in a cubicle or in a chaotic room full of customers.

"A great moment of service starts simply. You do your job and then, for some inexplicable reason, you go the extra mile for someone. You do something extra nice for a co-worker. You give generously of yourself (with a peaceful humility that comes so easily it even shocks yourself) to a client or customer. You do this thing not because you have to, but because you want to. You do this great thing at work because it *feels* right.

And then *it* happens. A stillness comes over you. The mind clears of useless, back-talking chatter. You feel a lift. You feel happy. For an instance, you feel free. You want to do a victory dance.

This is what living a life of service is all about. **The more you give, the more you get.**

If I spend all my time looking out for everyone else, who's going to look out for me?

Being of service is a difficult thing. Believe me, I know. It's been my job for almost twenty years. It's not impossible to find myself surrounded by people with big egos and angry hearts who will do wildly cruel and devious things just to mess with me. The people who like to make others feel small to boost themselves up are the biggest challenge to the practice of mindful service. Because being of service to jerks, blowhards, meanies, and self-obsessed people makes the proposition *the key to life is service* seem impossible.

But the reason why I think it's important to share with you this idea of being of service to others is because I think it really is the key to finding happiness. The key might be simple but the act of using it is hard.

Here's the thing. Ever since divine inspiration came to visit during nap time, I've noticed I've had more and more opportunities to do little things for other people. Whenever my thinking gets chaotic or my motives seem to be a little off, I jump into action. I put aside my fears, concerns, and mind chatter and remember to put my focus on service. Rather than mope or feel bad for myself, I open the door for strangers. I greet fellow joggers *good morning* as I pass by them on my run. I pack snacks for my husband before he goes to work. I call friends and listen to what's happening in their lives (rather than complain about mine).

And you know what? Being of service to others makes me happy; really happy.

The more we give ourselves, it seems, the more we get. I'm starting to realize that the act of being of service to others is like making a deposit in someone else's bank account and still getting dividends. I'm not sure what kind of banking system that's called, but I like the way it works. Being of service to others is an investment in our future happiness.

I had a dream

I had a dream, and in it I saw what the world could look like if we all worked for the happiness of others first. It was beautiful!

So thank you for sticking around and reading these words. I really appreciate you taking the time and reading this stuff. What you're doing is being of service to me and I appreciate it. I hope it gave something back to you in return.

How has the humble act of taking care of another person's needs before your own made a difference in your life?"

CHAPTER FOUR

PROTECTION

In the field of law enforcement, we are sworn to protect life and property. Officers do this without reservation in most cases because it's what they signed up for; they understand the risks that are associated with the profession. It may be a "No Brainer" to be willing to protect the things that you personally own, but to put your life on the line for the property and lives of others is something all together different; yet there are those that take on this responsibility daily.

Men and women in our armed forces who enlist to secure our freedom and the life that we enjoy in these United States of America. Those who serve in faraway lands, and those who secure our borders here on the home front.

Policemen and women who pledge to protect your assets when you are away from home and protect your life while you are going about your day to day routine. What about fathers and mothers looking out for their children, or a big brother or sister being on the ready to take up for, and protect a younger sibling? All of these are instances of protection. You see, protection is a part of life. There is something that is inherently in the DNA of all creation that causes us to protect life and what belongs to us.

However as we deal with the topic of Red, White, and True, living your faith in the workplace in America, I want to move beyond the protection of life and property in the generic sense and explore others areas of protection. I want to talk about the protection of our hearts, minds, and souls.

We must guard these with everything that we have, even in the workplace. Have you ever noticed how someone can go to church on Sunday and when they get to work on Monday it seems as if there is no evidence that there was any type of Sunday experience? To be able to protect you must first have a relationship with God through His Son Jesus Christ. There are many who just go through the motions and think that it is enough, I submit to you that it is not enough. All of us who are or have been in the workplace can relate to the fact that they have encountered a fellow co-worker or maybe it was themselves who was in a bad mood, irritable, and it just brought the whole place down. Well this is part of living your faith in the workplace. We all have days when we might not feel up to par and we all go through one thing or another in life, that is why it's so important to know that we have a protector who watches over us and is there for us. The enemy wants us to act out of character when we are in the workplace, I know, I've been there. In church on Sunday and then Monday comes and so does the foul mouth, the jokes, and the allowing of Satan to dominate our life and completely jeopardize our witness.

We must be sincere and pray that our witness is protected from the enemy. But we have a part to play in that protection. You see, we must be real with God and ourselves, understanding that there just might be some relationships in the workplace that we have to let go of, especially if we know that we are not strong enough to be around them and not be negatively influenced by them. This has nothing to do with loving them; we must learn to love everyone even if we might not like what they are doing. What this is about is living effective lives in the presence of God and others. America is in dire need of people that will take a stand and live for God in the workplace. First of all, because it isthe right thing to do. Secondly, because it is a place where we can have a great impact of masses of people; this is due to the fact that there are more and more people in the work place at this present time.

We are at a time in our history when more and more people find themselves returning to work, some for the opportunity to stay active, others to be able to make ends meet and live. Either way, there are more people, so there are also more chances to impact someone's life. Too many people who say that they have a relationship with Christ don't let it show while they are at work; it is as if they are seemingly ashamed of the Lord and only want to be involved with Him on a Sunday basis while they are confined within the walls of a church building. **We must do more! We have to do more!** Trust me; I know how we can all look as though we have it all together when truly we are hurting and going through difficult times. In my last book I talked about being light. We must step up and protect our faith. It starts with each of us individually, and then as a body.

Protect your mind. While you are at work or at home, you must protect your mind. The enemy wants to influence your mind by having you to watch all kinds of things and listen to all kind of crazy things. You can ask God to keep you, but it won't happen if you are not willing to do the things that are needed to be done in your life. Many watch all kinds of garbage on television and then wonder why they are not effective in the area of providing positive influence in the workplace. When you are born again, you are made alive in Christ but the enemy wants you to walk the way that you use to walk. Listen to what the scripture says; *"And you He made alive, who were dead in trespasses and sins, in which you once walked according to the course of this world, according to the prince of the power of the air, the spirit who now works in the sons of disobedience"(Ephesians 2:1-2)*

So, we must guard our minds and stay positive and depend on the Word of God to help keep us even in the workplace. Someone will always be going through something and will need an encouraging word. Being able to quote a scripture is not enough, and it is really sad when someone discounts the words that come from you simply because of the life that you portrait in front of them. I have heard people talk about the Lord or the bible in one breath and the very next moment use profanity in the same conversation. This type of thing hinders and destroys a testimony. If we need our minds guarded, it is even more so in the workplace. We spend eight or more hours a day on our jobs, having interaction with others all the time, so we need to understand that not only do we have a responsibility for our mind, but can influence the minds of others as well.

Living lives that bring honor to God is a wonderful privilege that we have; understand this; **GOD WANTS TO USE YOU IN THE WORKPLACE!** He has a wonderful plan for your life and has a purpose that is uniquely yours; you were created for His purpose.

Protect your heart. I encourage you to protect your natural heart with healthy eating, exercise and regularly scheduled check- ups, but also your heart which is your spirit. There are many things or devices that the enemy puts in the path. It may be with your supervisor or a fellow worker, it may be through a customer or a vendor, remember Satan does not play by the rules and if allowed he will use anyone or anything to get to you.

He wants to get you to move out of your Christian character and make a mockery of God and anything that is attached to God. When we are going through something ourselves the best thing to do is look up to God who is the author and finisher of our faith. Not when we get a chance at home or at church, but right there where we are on the job. This is one of the reasons why meditation is so important. There is a great benefit of learning the scriptures, to have something on the inside that we can draw from or go to in the time of need.

We have all had those days at work where we felt overwhelmed and overworked. Those days when we put our head in our hands and wonder when will this day be over. I can assure you that these are times when the enemy will try hardest to come against you, to turn you to something that is worldly and not of God or His will. It is in these times that we need to look to the spirit man and God's word, for as the Apostle Paul declares in the letter the church at Rome; ***"For to be carnally minded is death; but to be spiritually minded is life and peace"(Romans 8:6).*** If you are a child of God, there is no reason to turn to carnal thinking when you are faced with some type of adversity in the workplace. This is a time to allow your heart to be filled with the grace of God and the comfort that only the Holy Spirit can provide.

Protect your soul. When you are at work, remember that you are not taking a break from being a child of God. There are those who act as if they are in an intermission when they are away from the church house. **Let's wake up!** Satan does not take time off. He is on the job at all times and he wants to influence you so that you want be on your job in the kingdom. There is a heaven and there is a hell. One was not made for us; hell was created for Satan and his followers. We cannot afford to take a break from kingdom living, our souls are at stake. It is not enough to be content with the saying "I gave my life to God at an early age" and think that will somehow be all that is required of us.

I want to encourage you to live lives of excellence, and not settle for anything that the enemy wants to give you. Our Heavenly Father wants us to succeed in every aspect of our lives. He wants us to be living testimonies at the workplace and in the marketplace. Jesus said; *"The thief does not come except to steal, kill, and to destroy. I have come that they may have life, and that they may have it more abundantly."(John 10:10)* Again; He wants you to be victorious and enjoy abundant living in every aspect of your life!

So what am I saying? I'm saying that in many careers, especially law enforcement, we train in the area of defensive tactics for safety, for protection, that we may remain focused and be able to defend against those who would attack or try to harm us. This is from a physical and mental standpoint; but we should make sure that we have spiritual defensive tactics as well, and it comes from applying the word of God to our lives at all times, including the workplace.

"To everything there is a season, a time for every purpose under heaven; A time to be born, and a time to die; A time to plant, and a time to pluck up what is planted; A time to kill, and a time to heal; A time to break down, and a time to build up; A time to weep, and a time to laugh; A time to mourn, and a time to dance; A time to cast away stones, and a time to gather stones; A time to embrace, and a time to refrain from embracing; A time to gain, and a time to lose; A time to keep, and a time to throw away; A time to tear, and a time to sew; A time to keep silence, and a time to speak; A time to love, and a time to hate; A time of war, and a time of peace. What profit has the worker from that in which he labors?"

(Ecclesiastes 3:1-9)

SECTION III

OUR POSITION

CHAPTER FIVE

POLITICALLY
CORRECT?

Wikipedia defines politically correctness as: A term which denotes language, ideas, policies and behavior seen as seeking to minimize social and institutional offense in occupational, gender, racial, cultural, sexual orientation, certain other religious beliefs or ideologies, disability, and age related contexts, and, as purported by the term, doing so to an excessive extent.

Here we are. At the "meat and potatoes" of the message of, living your faith in the workplace in America. The scripture states, "To everything there is a season." To say that this country is in the season of need is a great understatement. America has become asphyxiated with being politically correct rather than being pleasing to God. We live here in this great nation, with great pride and tradition, and patriotism, but as a nation we have moved further away from the values and principles of God's holy word. We have become a complacent people who seemingly make every attempt to please man instead of God. If you are a believer, it's time to step up to the plate and show it. Again we are a nation in desperate need of revival. I know that I am by no means the only one who sees and understands this. I continue to hear the pledge of allegiance being recited "One nation under God" and to the disdain of some, we continue to spend currency with "In God we trust" printed on it.

It seems as if it is all just a show now. It's just a formality to get a meeting started or a game underway. WHERE ARE THE SAINTS OF GOD? Many are too busy being politically correct; they don't want to offend anyone so they adhere to the term "separation of church and state". Their actions, and their language, as it relates to their faith are kept in its "proper place" the church house on Sunday and possibly on Wednesday. How do we as a nation expect God to bless us when we go contrary to the laws and judgments He has given? We have to be bold in the face of adversity and stand on the word of God. We cannot afford to travel a road where we are continuously trying to be men pleasers.

Peter and the apostles were faced with similar challenges in the bible days. They were preaching and teaching the doctrine of Christ and came against opposition, but I really like what is recorded in the book of Acts, the fifth chapter and verse twenty-nine. They were brought before the high priest and council and he stated, *"Did we not strictly command you not to teach in this name (Jesus)? Then Peter and the other apostles answered and said; "We ought to obey God rather than men."(Acts 5: 28-29)* Wow! What boldness, you see these men had just been released from prison for living their faith and were not afraid of going back for the gospel's sake. They did all of this under the unction or direction of the Holy Spirit, and that same Spirit is available to you and me today.

It's time out for political correctness, souls are at stake. And this is particularly true for our younger generation. They are being brought up to believe right is wrong and wrong is right. They are being brainwashed into believing that anything goes in America, and it's all good. Well, it's not all good. Look at the economy, look at the current events in the news, look at the political climate; I assure you it's not all good. This is a nation that is out of control, starting from the White House and unfortunately the Church House. Why? Because many are afraid to take a stand for righteousness; especially in the workplace. In this country we are too afraid of offending someone with our righteous views. NEWS FLASH! Why is it that the pendulum seems to swing only to one side? What about all of the things that offend me and other believers? Why is it that we have to take any and everything and when we speak our mind and the word of God then someone is offended and we are censored?

You see, in today's time a joke on the internet or email can have its run throughout the office, but often times when you try to send something about Jesus or biblical content you are cut off and get responses like "this recipient cannot receive material with this content". I realize that this is one form of expression, but it is an increasing communication medium used by millions of people. What are we as a nation afraid of? You often here the term ,"their rights". This group's rights and that group's rights; what about the believer's rights? So often it seems as though everyone's rights are looked after except the Christian's. With all this said; we don't have an excuse to be complacent in our faith. We must stand and be courageous in the face of adversity and live for Father that loves us unconditionally.

One day I received an email stating that Chaplains of a police department in North Carolina can no longer use the name of Jesus in their official meeting invocations. America, this is where we are, yet we want the blessings of God. Listen to me, to say a prayer and not close it in Jesus' name is like having a check but there is no signature on it. Without the signature it is no good, I don't care how much it is for, without the signature it is just another piece of paper. Will you give in to the arena of political correctness or will you stand up for the Lord Jesus Christ? The Scriptures Declare:

"Do not fret because of evil doers, nor be envious of the workers of iniquity. For they shall be soon cut down like the grass, And whither as the green herb. Trust in the Lord, and do good; Dwell in the land, and feed on His faithfulness. Delight yourself also

in the Lord, And He shall give you the desires of your heart. Commit your way to the Lord, Trust also in Him, and He shall bring forth your righteousness as the light. And your justice as the noonday." (Psalm 37:1-6)

CHAPTER SIX
PRAISER

As you read this book I don't know if you are at work, at home, or even possibly at church; but wherever you are, you need to praise God. The fact that you are able to read this lets me know that you are being blessed by God. Why wait until Sunday to give Him the praise? Worship Him right now! If it means that you have to put this book down, give Him the praise! He has been good, He is good, and He will always be good. He has done so much for you. I know he has been good to me. "IF IT HAD NOT BEEN FOR THE LORD THAT WAS ON MY SIDE, WHERE WOULD I BE"? Where would you be? Yet in the context of this writing, many seem to forget what the Lord has done in their life. When they are on their blessed jobs, they act like they are playing the game of quiet mouse when it comes to them being a witness for the Lord Jesus. They think more about the job than the one who allowed them to get the job.

They may think that they got employment on their own merit, maybe because of their intellect or education; maybe because of someone they knew at the workplace or in the community, maybe someone put in a good word for you. Whatever the case, I can tell you that it was the Lord who blessed you. So you ought to bless Him and praise Him wherever you are; even on the job. Listen to the Psalmist David; *"I will bless the Lord at all times; His praise shall continually be in my mouth. My soul shall make its boast in the Lord." (Psalm 34:1-2).* With all of the stressors and distractions in the workplace, praising Him will help keep you focused and will keep you content as you go through the work day. I know, because it works for me. There are times when we are bombarded by one thing or another and we find ourselves getting frustrated like anyone else, but it's in those times that I am reminded of the words of the psalmist and began to praise God all the more. And in the process I try my best to encourage someone else along the way.

I am not ashamed of the gospel of Jesus Christ! I realize that it is He that keeps me and sustains me, so I have to praise Him. That is the way I start my work day, by worshiping and praising Him and He helps me to get through every day without being overwhelmed and beaten down. I am strengthened by the Holy Spirit's power and comfort. When you are in the workplace I know that you are presented with all types of challenges and situations and it is because of this that you need to praise God and be refreshed in the process. Going further in this passage of Psalm 34 it is recorded;

"Oh magnify the Lord with me, And let us exalt His name together. I sought the Lord, and He heard me and delivered me from all my fears. They looked to Him and were radiant, and their faces were not ashamed. This poor man cried out, and the Lord heard him, and saved him out of all of his troubles. The angel of the Lord encamps all around those who fear Him, and delivers them. Oh, taste and see that the Lord is good; blessed is the man who trust in Him! Oh, fear the Lord, you His saints! There is no want to those who fear Him. The young lions lack and suffer hunger; But those who seek the Lord shall not lack any good thing." (Psalm 34:3-10) Did you get that? There is no want to those that fear Him; even in the workplace. You have the ability and authority in the Lord to have peace, joy and contentment while you are on the job. The problem with many is that they try their best to keep some type of separation between their work and their faith. The psalmist didn't say I will bless the Lord sometimes, part of the time, but he said at ALL TIMES. Ask yourself this question; what would my workplace be like if those that proclaim they have a relationship with God would take a stand and operate in and share their faith? Now ask this question; what would my workplace be like if I would live out my faith there? Again, maybe you're not at

church or at a revival that is much needed, but at work. I declare to you that the work of God is not bound. So I give you a charge to: *"Make a joyful shout to the Lord, all you lands! Serve the Lord with gladness; Come before His presence with singing. Know that the Lord, He is God; it is He who has made us, and not we ourselves; We are His people and the sheep of His pasture. Enter into His gates with thanksgiving, and into His courts with praise. Be thankful to Him, and bless His name. For the Lord is good; His mercy is everlasting, and His truth endures to all generations." (Psalm 100)*

This should be the mindset of the believer in the workplace. Trust the Lord in this and see if He won't bless you and make your day more refreshing and productive. Try it!

You see His mercy is everlasting, and you will benefit greatly from living out your faith instead of having it all bottled up. Not only will you be blessed, but I guarantee you will bless others also. We don't know all of the trails, or the hurts and pains that people are experiencing from day to day; what I do know is that God is a lifter of bowed heads, even when the person(s) are not showing it outwardly. Someone can draw strength and encouragement from you when you are praising God, and some just can't understand how you are able to be so upbeat and positive. This is that opportunity to let them know, "Greater is He that is in me, than he that is in the world." All of the praise and glory goes to God!

Praise must become who you are. By this I mean; you must have a heart to praise, an attitude if you will. The attitude that says, in the midst of everything that's going on here, I will praise the Lord. When people are down and want to bring you down with them, the attitude must be I will praise the Lord. When things are not going the way you want them to go, the attitude must be I will praise the Lord. You may be going through some pain yourself, but you have to praise Him through your pain, and like Nehemiah declare that the "Joy of the Lord is my strength!" I'm not saying that this is always easy, but it is worth it.

Listen, you can praise God in every aspect of your life. Even within your occupation you can bring honor to the Lord by the life that you live and the service that you give. Praise will help you get through a trying day. Praise will allow you to be in a position to help somebody else. Praise will allow you to be elevated in your position, and it will make it so that you will be able to see the purpose of challenging times with clarity, and be at peace in the midst of your enemies. Consider this praise; *"The Lord lives! Blessed be my rock! Let the God of my salvation be exalted. It is God who avenges me, and subdues the people under me. He delivers me from my enemies. You also lift me up above those who rise against me; You have delivered me from the violent man. Therefore I will give thanks to You, O Lord, among the Gentiles, and sing praises to Your name." (Psalm 18:46-50)* Are you a praiser?

"Behold, this day I am going the way of all the earth. And you know in all your hearts and in all your souls that not one thing has failed of all the good things which the Lord your God spoke concerning you. All have come to pass for you, and not one word of them has failed."

(Joshua 23:14)

SECTION IV

OUR PROMISE

CHAPTER SEVEN

EARTHLY REWARDS

You might ask yourself, what is all of this for? What good does it do? What does all of this hold for me? In this chapter I would like to deal with the promises that are there for those who have a personal relationship with Jesus Christ, and are not ashamed of Him no matter where they are, the workplace included. There are so many promises given to the Body of Christ. We will explore the earthly rewards in this chapter, and the eternal rewards in the next chapter.

First we must understand and believe what the word says about God. As recorded in the Old Testament scripture; *"God is not a man, that He should lie, Nor the son of man, that He should repent. Has He said, and will He not do it? Or has He spoken, and will he not make it good?"(Numbers 23:19)* Did you get that? What God says is fact, it's absolute, He cannot lie. This world was created by what He said. Man was created because He said; *"let Us make man in Our image, according to Our likeness;" (Genesis 1:26)* so, in that He created us in His image, He gave man dominion over everything on the earth, but because of disobedience and sin man forfeited or yielded the dominion into the hands of the enemy, Satan. But God had a plan to redeem and restore man, and it came in the perfected plan of Jesus Christ. You may ask, what kind of earthly promises are connected with Jesus? Well, through a relationship with Him, we are brought into a better position and place even in this earth. For example, we are promised blessings because of our obedience to Him.

[1] "Now it shall come to pass, if you diligently obey the voice of the LORD your God, to observe carefully all His commandments which I command you today, that the LORD your God will set you high above all nations of the earth.

2 And all these blessings shall come upon you and overtake you, because you obey the voice of the LORD your God:

3 Blessed shall you be in the city, and blessed shall you be in the country.

4 Blessed shall be the fruit of your body, the produce of your ground and the increase of your herds, the increase of your cattle and the offspring of your flocks.

5 Blessed shall be your basket and your kneading bowl.

6 Blessed shall you be when you come in, and blessed shall you be when you go out.

7 The LORD will cause your enemies who rise against you to be defeated before your face; they shall come out against you one way and flee before you seven ways.

8 The LORD will command the blessing on you in your storehouses and in all to which you set your hand, and He will bless you in the land which the LORD your God is giving you.

9 The LORD will establish you as a holy people to Himself, just as He has sworn to you, if you keep the commandments of the LORD your God and walk in His ways.

10 Then all peoples of the earth shall see that you are called by the name of the LORD, and they shall be afraid of you.

¹¹ And the LORD will grant you plenty of goods, in the fruit of your body, in the increase of your livestock, and in the produce of your ground in the land of which the LORD swore to your fathers to give you.

¹² The LORD will open to you His good treasure, the heavens, to give the rain to your land in its season, and to bless all the work of your hand. You shall lend to many nations, but you shall not borrow.

¹³ And the LORD will make you the head and not the tail; you shall be above only, and not be beneath, if you heed the commandments of the LORD your God, which I command you today, and are careful to observe them.

¹⁴ So you shall not turn aside from any of the words which I command you this day, to the right or the left, to go after other gods to serve them." (Deuteronomy 28:1-14)

What a word of promise! Not in the bye and bye, but right now. God has these promises along with others that are for those that love Him and have a relationship with Him, through His Son. The head and not the tail; above and not beneath, man that's awesome news to me that wherever I am I have these promises, even when I'm at work. I know that there are times when the day is not going the way you would want it to go at work, and something or someone has you at the point where you feel like "putting your faith on the shelf" as I have heard it said; but we must realize that one of the promises of the Lord that we have is that He will never leave us, nor forsake us. In those times when our day is hectic and we're on edge, we must remember that He is there to give us the peace and whatever we need to make it through. Being a child of God has its privileges' and He didn't give His Son to die so we could have miserable lives in the workplace. The workplace is another stage or arena, if you will that we have to demonstrate or exercise our faith. It is a place of opportunity. Not only to make an income, but to share the glorious life and love of our savior Jesus Christ. This relationship must be evident in the workplace. Listen to the words of Christ, *"I am the true vine, and My Father is the vinedresser. Every branch in Me that does not bear fruit He takes away; and every branch that bears fruit He prunes, that it may bear more fruit. You are already clean because of the word which I have spoken to you. Abide in Me, and I in you. As the branch cannot bear fruit of itself, unless it abides in the vine, neither can you, unless you abide in Me. I am the vine, you are the branches. He who abides in Me, and I in him bears much fruit; for without Me you can do nothing. If anyone does not abide in Me, he is cast out as a branch and is withered; and they gather them and throw them into the fire, and they are burned. If you abide in Me, and My words abide in you, you will ask what you desire, and it shall be done for you." (John 15:1-7)*

We must understand that this is not just reserved for Sunday morning, or related to quote, "church things." For, our everyday lives are a part of our relationship with Christ and that relationship should be reflected at all times. Jesus continued in verse 11 saying; *"These things I have spoken to you, that My joy may remain in you, and that your joy may be full."* That's why it bothers me to hear a lot of complaining in the workplace, especially among those who profess to have a relationship with Christ. One of the promises we have is joy. Full joy, that is visible. Joy that is expressed and share with others. Living out your faith in the workplace means to be an encourager to them that need encouragement. To spread some cheer to them who are down, and to give hope to them that need it.

One thing that is needful is; our minds have to be committed to Christ continually. Another promise is peace. God says that He would keep you in perfect peace, if your mind is stayed on Him. This means that whatever we go through, we can have peace in the midst of it because we are connected with the source of true peace. There are and will be those who scratch their heads in amazement when they see you at peace, when they see a storm all around you.

Joy and peace in the midst of your storm; wow! Look at the promises and blessings that we have here on earth. What I have come to know is; there will be those that like you and those that don't for whatever reason in the workplace. But we must live by and in the promises at all times so that the Lord may be glorified in us and that we might win someone to a blessed relationship with Him. We will all go through some tribulations in life, but we must hold fast to the words of Christ who says; *"These things I have spoken to you, that in Me you may have peace. In the world you will have tribulation; but be of good cheer, I have overcome the world." (John 16:33)* Praise God!

So we must identify those areas where we need help and bring them before the alter of the Lord and pray that we may receive what we need in Him to be victorious in our lives, and sow the right seeds that are needed, so that we might produce good fruit. Remember, He says; he who abides in Me and I in him, bears much fruit. That is not a suggestion; it's a fact and a promise.

We also have the promise of peace with God. Many believe that this is only possible when we get to heaven, but this is possible right here on earth. Let's look at a very powerful passage of scripture found in the Apostle Paul's writing to the church at Rome. *"Therefore, having been justified by faith, we have peace with God through our Lord Jesus Christ, through whom also we have access by faith into this grace in which we stand, and rejoice in the hope of the glory of God. And not only that, but we also glory in tribulations, knowing that tribulation produces perseverance; and perseverance, character; and character, hope. Now hope does not disappoint, because the love of God has been poured out in our hearts by the Holy Spirit who was given to us. For when we were still without strength, in due time Christ died for the ungodly. For scarcely for a righteous man will one die; yet perhaps for a good man someone would even dare to die. But God demonstrated His own love toward us that while we were still sinners, Christ died for us." (Romans 5:1-8)*

Glory! Do you understand that the promise of peace with God is through His Son Jesus Christ and one of the promises that we have is access to Him, because He said "whosoever will let him come", that means you and me. We all will go through tribulations, but He says that we glory in them knowing that it produces perseverance, which produces character, which brings hope that does not disappoint because the Holy Spirit has poured the love of God into our hearts. This is something that we really need to feast on and meditate on especially while we are in the workplace.

CHAPTER EIGHT

ETERNAL REWARDS

"For God so loved the world that He gave His only begotten Son, that whoever believes in Him should not perish but have everlasting life. For God did not send His Son into the world to condemn the world, but that the world through Him might be saved."

(John 3:16-17)

When we are born, we are born into eternity. The physical body will lie down or, to put it another way, we will experience a physical death, but our soul will experience either eternal life or eternal damnation or death. There are many promises that we have regarding the eternal. One of the most read or quoted passages of scripture that we most often hear at funeral services is St. John 14 which states; *" Let not your heart be troubled; you believe in God, believe also in Me. In My Father's house are many mansions; if it were not so, I would have told you. I go to prepare a place for you. And if I go and prepare a place for you, I will come again and receive you to Myself; that where I am, there you may be also." (John 14:1-3)* and although we hear this most often in situations concerning the dead, the passage itself speaks to life eternal.

You may ask yourself, why does all this matter? Who really cares if I'm living a God centered life in the workplace? What do I have to gain by it? I have already shared some of the benefits that you can experience on earth because of a personal relationship with Christ and living a life that is pleasing to Him. But to think of life everlasting and all of the eternal blessings that are a part of that relationship is what we gain. Take a look around you; with all of the chaos that is surrounding us now, surely one cannot think or feel that this is all there is. Murder, suicide, shootings and stabbings every night, infants and toddlers being left in hot vehicles that succumb to the heat, beatings, stealing, war. Not to mention the economy and the unemployment rate. Surely this is not all there is to life.

I submit to you; there is so much more in store for those that love the Lord! There are many that believe that this present world is all we have. So, why would anyone, especially those with that same mindset, not seek something better? My friends, there is something that is so much better.

Listen to John in the book of Revelation; *"And I saw a new heaven and a new earth, for the first heaven and the first earth had passed away. Also there was no more sea. Then I John, saw the holy city, New Jerusalem, coming down out of heaven from God, prepared as a bride adorned for her husband. And I heard a loud voice from heaven saying, "Behold the tabernacle of God is with men, and He will dwell with them, and they shall be His people, and God Himself will be with them and be their God. And God will wipe away every tear from their eyes; there shall be no more death, nor sorrow, nor crying; and there shall be no more pain, for the former things have passed away. Then He who sat on the throne said, "Behold, I make all things new." And He said to me, "Write, for these words are true and faithful." And He said to me, "It is done! I am the Alpha and the Omega, the Beginning and the End. I will give of the fountain of the water of life freely to him who thirsts. "He who overcomes shall inherit all things, and I will be his God and he shall be My son." (Revelation 21:1-7)*

No death, no sorrow, no crying, and no pain, let's consider just these four things right now. First the ability to live forever, secondly, everyone has experienced some type of sorrow, but the promise we have as it relates to the eternal, is that we will no longer endure any sorrow. There will only be peace. Oh the tears we shed in this life, but there will be no more crying in heaven. And no more pain, but everlasting joy!

I don't know what you are going through at this moment, but God knows and He has prepared a place and made a way for us to have relief from all of the pressures and trials of life in this present world. A fallen world that is becoming more vile with each passing day. In heaven we will be eternally free from all such things, and will be able to experience a peace like none other. How long will this last? The answer is, forever. Let's look further into this book of Revelation, John says; *"And he showed me a pure river of water of life, clear as crystal, proceeding from the throne of God and of the Lamb. In the middle of its street, and on either side of the river, was the tree of life, which bore twelve fruits, each tree yielding its fruit every month. And the leaves of the tree were for the healing of the nations. And there shall be no more curse, but the throne of God and of the Lamb shall be in it, and His servants shall serve Him. They shall see His face, and His name shall be on their foreheads. And there shall be no night there: they need no lamp nor light of the sun, for the Lord God gives them light. And they shall reign forever and ever. Then he said to me, "these words are faithful and true." And the Lord God of the holy prophets sent His angel to show His servants the things that must shortly take place. "Behold, I am coming quickly! Blessed is he who keeps the words of the prophecy of this book." (Revelation 22:1-7)*

All of this is a part of the eternal promise that we have from our creator. A creator who loves us unconditionally so much that He gave His son to die a horrible death for our sin. Why? Because He wanted eternal fellowship with mankind who was created in His very image, so He has laid out the perfect plan, through a perfect sacrifice, and prepared the perfect place. When we really take a look at all of this, if we are honest, we know that there is no comparison with life as we now know it, and life everlasting. Know this, heaven is a real place, it is not just a metaphor or some mystical place that we can only read or dream about. Real blood was shed so that we could have an opportunity to make it there.

Think about it for a moment. Name something you have or had that you thought would be forever, whether an object or a person, nothing on this earth is eternal. Eternity is in the hands of the one who created it. I know Him to be God! Not a god, or some god, but The GOD of all creation, and He has Promised that through His Son I, or I should say we, can live forever.

CONCLUSION

What does it all mean? Given the current state of our country; all of the shootings and seemingly no regard for life, the complacency and the cynicism. This volume is a challenge to be whom and what we are called to be, not just in the church house, but everywhere we go and especially in the workplace. Most of us spend far more time at our place of employment than we do at the church or even at home. And given some of the current state of affairs within the church many are leaving or giving up on the why part of being faithful, committed, and dedicated while they are at their employment.

Let's think for a minute, we are in the wake of another school tragedy that not only took lives, but innocent lives of children just starting out in life. There is no sense to make of it, so I dare not try. But when tragedy like that happens, it somehow seems easy to point the finger and blame God. Why should I live for Him? Where was He during that time? The answer that I have is He was right where He always is and in His permissive will, yes He allows bad things to happen in this fallen world. Yet, He is still worthy of all of our praise. His glory and honor still remain and His grace is sufficient for us during the tough times in our lives. Can we rise up and be witnesses that are not ashamed? Can we live out our testimony in the workplace and in the world and not just at one of the church meetings? The Lord has been and is faithful to us, I can assure you of that. So we need to acknowledge Him with the fruit of our lives. With the fruit of our lips, we should declare that He is Lord of our lives and invite others to share in that same experience. I know that times are tough, and that there are so many things happening all over this world, but there is good news also. Just because it doesn't get the same media exposure as the bad news or the same billing so to speak, I declare to you that The Holy Spirit is at work in the lives of those who have surrendered their life to the Lord Jesus Christ. I have found that my day is better in the workplace when I start it off with prayer and meditation. Things can become hectic at work for many of us, and I know that we are often challenged to smile in the midst of it all, but it is worth it knowing that the Lord has our backs.

The Apostle Paul states it beautifully in the book of acts when he writes; *"And see, now I go bound in the spirit to Jerusalem, not knowing the things that will happen to me there, except that the Holy Spirit testifies in every city, saying that chains and tribulations await me. But none of these things move me; nor do I count my life dear to myself, so that I may finish my race with joy, and the ministry which I received from the Lord Jesus, to testify to the gospel of grace of God."(Acts 20:22-24)* AMEN!

We cannot be moved from our faith when things are not going the way we would want them to go in our daily lives, and especially at the workplace. Our continued focus should be on impacting the lives of others for good. Don't kid yourself, when you make a declaration that you are a Christian, people will take notice and watch to see how you respond in certain situations. Let's make sure that we represent Christ well, because He is seated on the right side of the Father, representing us very well.

PRAYER

My heavenly Father, the God of all hope. I thank you for filling me with your joy and peace as I believe in you. I overflow with hope through the Holy Spirit who is within me. In Him, I am full of goodness, knowledgeable and able to teach others the things that I know. Thank you Father for always being there for me when I call, I pray for your forgiveness where I have felled you and sinned against you. I stand on your word that you are faithful and just to forgive, and cleanse me from all unrighteousness. I pray for others; for those that are reading this book right now, I pray that you will bless them and meet every need that they have in their life, in the Name of Jesus. I pray for co-workers, and for brothers and sisters in Christ everywhere, and especially those that contend in the workplace in America. We have so much to be thankful for and still there is so much work to be done here when I think of the gospel being not only preached but lived. I pray for those that are challenged everyday at their place of employment to take a stand and be true to who you have called them to be. To be true ambassadors of the kingdom, and represent it and you with faithful service and obedience until you call and say well done. Wherever you allow us to go Lord, I pray that we will take with us, the abundant blessings of the gospel and know that the awareness of your presence, love, and peace remains with us at all times. In Jesus Name, Amen!

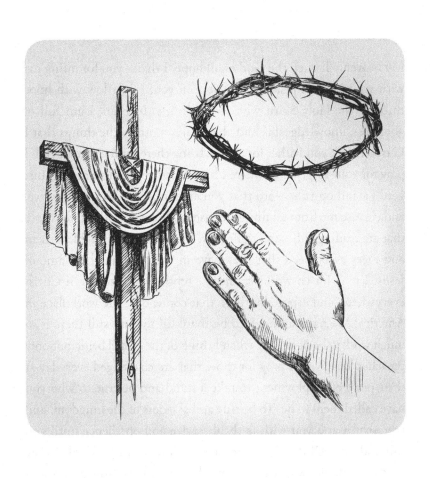

RED

Red represents our sins, all of our iniquity, all of our transgressions against a Holy God who created us in His image. Red represents mans fall in the Garden of Eden, and how our dominion was forfeited. It represents generation after generation of failing, of turning our backs on the one who loves us most. But red also represents the blood of Christ, which cleanses us from all sin, a perfect sacrifice, an unblemished atonement. As the word declares, He who knew no sin became sin, that we might be made the righteousness of God in Christ Jesus. It also says that without the shedding of blood, there is no remission for sin. 1John states; *"But if we walk in the light as He is in the light, we have fellowship with one another, and the blood of Jesus Christ His Son cleanses us from all sin."(1John 1:7)*

WHITE

White represents purity. It represents cleanliness, and how we are after we have been washed in the blood of the lamb. One of the scriptures that come to mind at this time and states it beautifully is: Psalm 51. Listen; *"Have mercy upon me, O God, according to Your loving kindness; according to the multitude of Your tender mercies, Blot out my transgressions. Wash me thoroughly from my iniquity, and cleanse me from my sin. For I acknowledge my transgressions and my sin is always before me. Against You, You only, have I sinned, and done this evil in Your sight, that You may be found just when You speak, and blameless when You judge. Behold, I was brought forth in iniquity and in sin my mother conceived me. Behold, You desire truth in the inward parts, and in the hidden part You will make me to know wisdom. Purge me with hyssop, and I shall be clean; Wash me, and I shall be whiter than snow. Make me to hear joy and gladness, that the bones You have broken may rejoice. Hide Your face from my sins, and blot out all my iniquities. Create in me a clean heart, O God, and renew a steadfast spirit within me. Do not cast me away from Your presence, and do not take Your Holy Spirit from me. Restore to me the joy of Your salvation, and uphold me by Your generous Spirit. Then I will teach transgressors Your ways, and sinners shall be converted to You."(Psalm 51:1-13)*

TRUE

Being in accordance with the actual state or conditions; conforming to reality or fact. Real; genuine; authentic; sincere; not deceitful; firm in allegiance; loyal; faithful; steadfast: a true friend. Being or reflecting the essential or genuine character; exact; precise; accurate; correct; legitimate or rightful; reliable, unfailing, or sure.

God is true. God's word is true, God's judgments are true. God's promises are true. Christ is true. His life is true, His death was true, His resurrection is true, His testimony is true. The Holy Spirit is true. The Gospel is true. Jesus said; *"I am the way, the truth, and the life. No one comes to the Father except through Me." (John14:6)*

Regardless of how things may look or even appear, God is still on the throne, and Jesus is Lord of Lords, and King of all Kings. He is the Alpha and Omega, the beginning and the ending, the first and the last. And by Him all things exist. This is also true. Please get this in your spirit and you will be blessed forevermore. *"Most assuredly, I say to you, he who believes in Me, the works that I do he will do also; and greater works than these he will do, because I go to My Father. And whatever you ask in My name, that I will do, that the Father may be glorified in the Son. If you ask anything in My Name, I will do it."(John 14:12-14)* Glory to God! Hallelujah for the truth!

RESOURCES

www.ahdictionary.com American Heritage Dictionary

www.foodwoolf.com/2011/07live-a-life-of-service.html by: Food Woolf July2,2011

National Institute of Justice "Research in Brief" May 2000 "The Measurement of Police Integrity" by: Carl B. Klockers, Sanja Kanjak Ivkovich, William E. Harver, and Maria Haberfeld

www.llen.m.wikipedia.org

www.wisdomcommons.org/virtue/106reliability/lifestories

SPECIAL THANKS

I would like to give special thanks to all my brothers and sisters in the Law Enforcement community, especially to the men and women of the Mt. Juliet, TN. Police Department, whom I proudly serve as Chief. To the Mundy, and Musice families, the Wilson County Sheriff's Office, and to the citizens in whom we have the privilege of serving. Also to Mr. Jim Bradshaw for your help with this project, may God continue to bless each of you richly and may we all continue to strive for lives of excellence that are well pleasing to Him.

Visit James at:

www.jamesahambrick.com

Follow Him on:

Facebook, Twitter, Linkedin

NOTES